Jealousy or Envy: Is There a Killer in You?

Jealousy or Envy: Is There a Killer in You?

Stop the War Within and Be Set Free!

Linda Payton Thompson

Some quotes and scriptures were taken from the New Living Translation-TouchPoint Bible, King James Version Giant Print, and the Webster's New Collegiate Dictionary, A Merriam-Webster ®, Springfield, Massachusetts, USA, 1980 by G. & C. Merriam Co., Philippines Copyright 1980 by G & C Merriam Co.

New Living Translation, TouchPoint Bible (a quick study bible) 1996 by Tyndale House Publishers, Inc., Wheaton, Illinois 60189 all rights reserved TouchPoint Bible. Ed. Dr.V. Gilbert Beers and Ronald A. Beers. The New Living Translation ed. Wheaton: Tyndale House Publishers, Inc.

KJV Giant Print, personal Size Reference Bible Copyright 1994 by The Zondervan Corporation All right reserved

Unless otherwise stated Scriptures were taken from the New Living Translation.

Printed in the United States of America

Publishing services by Selah Publishing Group, LLC, Indiana. The views expressed or implied in this work do not necessarily reflect those of Selah Publishing Group.

ISBN: 1-58930-143-9
Library of Congress Control Number: 2004115041

I dedicate this book to my son, Lamont, and all of my nephews, nieces, and each reader. Since we all will be faced with tests and trials, I encourage each of you to be strong and look to God to help you through every problem and situation that you might encounter.

In Memory Of

This beloved book is in memory of those who slept away in Christ before its completion.

To my parents, David and Catherine Payton, who God allowed to bring me into this world for such a time as this to declare that Jesus is Lord over every situation. They taught me about unconditional love, doing the right thing, and being focused on my goals and not the crowd. I was always encouraged to do my best so I could at least say I tried.

To my sister, Brenda Payton, who was one of the best Kindergarten and First grade teachers in Pitt County. She was very creative and loved to read. She encouraged me to one day write a book so that others will know that God is greater than any test or trial that we can encounter. Although she is not here to read it, I know she is in heaven rejoicing over the many who will.

To my Cousin, Ann Robbins who always spoke of how God's love can get us through anything that we might encounter.

To my mother-in-law, Essie Thompson, who endured many tests and trials but knew that God was able to do anything but fail.

Acknowledgements

I would like to thank my Pastoral mentors, Dr. Bernard Grant and Sister Gloria Grant. I am very thankful to be a member of Showers of Blessing Christian Center in Goldsboro, North Carolina. It is due to their genuine love, concern, and devotion that has inspired me to step out in faith and write my first book. They encourage us to pursue our vision and goals in life. So many of the teachings have prompted me to believe that I can do anything if I trust and believe God. Dr. Grant's teachings such as: the "ABC'S of Faith", "Walking in Whole Life Prosperity", "Thinking Outside The Box", "Discovering Your Destiny In God", etc. have motivated and challenged me to get out of my comfort zone and to move toward God's greatness.

I would like to thank my husband Eddie and son Lamont for encouraging me to go for it and for telling me I could do it. I thank God for their love, encouragement and support throughout the process. I thank them for believing in me.

I give special thanks to my friend, Tina Williams, who has both prayed for me and with me as I have endured test and trials of persecution and rejection. She exemplifies what true friendship means.

Thanks to my friend, Grace Baker, who prays for me and always encourages me to be still and watch the Lord move. I also thank her prayer group for their prayers.

Acknowledgements

Thanks to my friends Carmen Williams, Joyace Ussin, and Dorothy for all of their prayers and support.

Thanks to all who will read my book and share information with others to bring about a positive change. I am very thankful for the connection that we have already made just by you taking the time to read my book.

I would like to thank Twla Sauls and Cora Allen for editing and proofreading my book.

I would like to thank my extended family for loving me; being proud of me and always making me feel special. I truly thank God for my brothers and sisters. I thank my in-laws for their love as well.

I would like to thank Selah Publishing Company for making my project a reality. A special thank you goes to Garlen for patiently guiding me through the process.

I would like to thank my former Pastor for the messages that he taught regarding being spiritually equipped for the trials and tests that we go through. So many messages have enabled me to press on and to outlast the persecution.

Most importantly of all, I would like to thank God, my Lord and saviour Jesus Christ, for giving me the grace to complete my first book. I am thankful for being obedient to this assignment so that God can bring forth his will for my life. I thank him for the boldness and confidence that he has given me to complete my project. I pray that he will create more love in everyone's heart and do something extra special and miraculous for each reader.

Contents

Foreword

by Eddie Thompson

My wife has devoted many years to the writing of her first book. She is truly gifted, dedicated, and concerned about the welfare of others. I strongly encourage each of you who read this book to tell a friend, coworker, family member and those who you come in contact with, what you have learned from reading this awesome book. It can change someone's outlook about the Killers that are within. I have witnessed Linda's constant focus as she concentrated and meditated on God's word. She didn't quit or give up when she was going through persecution. She endured every test and trial with victory. She didn't become bitter but better. I really admire her consistency and commitment to the things of God. Her greatest desire is to see people delivered from Jealousy and Envy and to exercise genuine love like never before. I recommend this book to everyone. I love you Linda and as always I wish you the best in all of your endeavors.

Your Mighty Man of God

Eddie Thompson

Foreword

by Tina Williams

The time has come that Jealousy and Envy, the Evil Twins, are exposed. I have seen the destructiveness of these two spirits. No one is better prepared to write on this subject than my dear friend and sister in the Lord, Linda Thompson. Through her own struggles, Linda has overcome what the devil meant for bad and the Lord has changed it into something good. I admired her steadfastness during the persecution she endured because the anointing on her life was so evident. A jealous spirit, however, does not play fair. It can use those closest to you to wound you and be a source of great pain. Now is the time for people to be set free and for this reason; this book was written. Oftentimes, Linda and I would discuss her manuscript and her greatest desire was always deliverance. This book is a must read for all of those who have been victimized by the spirits of Jealousy and Envy. It is also a must read for those who have these spirits working through them. It is only when sin is exposed that there can be true deliverance. I highly recommend this book because the body of Christ is getting ready to enter a season of full manifestation of all of God's promises. As believers, we can't afford to let these spirits run rampant in our homes, schools, churches, workplaces, etc. Christians must be on the front lines exposing anything that is contrary to the word of God.

It is my prayer that through the words on these pages that many eyes will be opened, knowledge increased, and freedom will prevail.

A genuine friend

Tina Williams

Introduction

The Killers I am referring to are Jealousy and Envy. Jealousy and Envy can hinder a person from being productive and happy in life. These are two of the most denied sins among people today, because they are too painful or shameful to admit or confess. These sins attack the inner man, his will and emotions, which can't be seen but can be displayed in many destructive ways. Many people will say I would never kill anyone; however, it doesn't always involve doing it with a gun or knife. It can be the use of the tongue, actions, and words that kill or destroy a person's feelings or reputation. Positive words have a positive effect and bring about life. Negative words have a negative effect and can bring about spiritual death to a person or situation. According to Proverbs 18:21, "Those who love to talk will experience the consequences, for the tongue can kill or nourish life"(NLT). Uncontrolled jealousy and envy have led some people to actual murder. This is often seen in Domestic Violence cases. We are now living in a time when people are being blessed more than ever, inspite of what is going on in the world today. On the other hand, there are those who are more stressed and frustrated than ever. It is very crucial that we keep our heart and mind right with a love and desire to see someone prosper and to not harbor negative thoughts in our mind and wish them evil or misfortune.

Introduction

Jealousy and envy can destroy a person's self-image or self-esteem. Self-esteem is how you feel about yourself. Everyone at some point has experienced jealousy to some degree either as a small child or an adult. The thought may have been just a passing thought. Jealousy is also present within families and this can bring about some destruction to the members. Families are being torn apart for this very reason. There are brothers and sisters who are growing further and further apart due to competitiveness.

I recall when I was growing up that my sister Brenda and I were very close. I was able to do a lot of things with her due to us being two years apart in age. However, I experienced my first significant encounter with jealousy when she graduated from high school and I was promoted to the 10th grade. After her graduation, her leaving and going to college meant I would be left at home and she would go off to meet new friends. It was a bad feeling for me because I was so used to being with her and I really depended on her in more ways than I imagined. However, this separation in my life gave me the opportunity to become more independent since my big sister was gone. I had to accept the fact that she was gone and be happy for her, because I knew my day was coming and I too would graduate and meet new people. My love for her helped me to cast away the feeling of jealousy I had regarding her leaving home. True love will not allow anyone to harm anyone else or try to hinder his or her progress.

Jealousy in any relationship is serious and can cause a lot of emotional pain. The ultimate experience is to be betrayed due to jealousy by those who are close to you, and those who are in your circle of friends and acquaintances. This can bring about the feelings of rejection and betrayal; however, when separation from certain people takes place it can be for one's own good or benefit so that one can grow into the things of God. It is well worth it. God will transform a person into something really beautiful.

Some Christians become jealous and envious because they feel that they are living holy or right and things should work out fast and in a hurry. Instead, it doesn't and then someone else gets what he or she wants. According to their inventory of someone else's life, it appears that the individual is not doing what is right nor living right, but somehow seems to be blessed. The person might not be a Christian or even a truly committed Christian and it just doesn't seem fair. We must be happy for others and cheer others on even when they may have something that we want or have accomplished something that we would like to accomplish. Too often, people are judged for what they may have without one knowing the private struggles of how they achieved success. People rarely take the time to inquire or ask how they accomplished their goals. Sometimes people can have a lot of things and still not be happy. It might seem like they have it all together but inside there's no peace or joy.

Always remember, just because someone is blessed doesn't mean they attained it easy. Normally, there is a lot of hard work and a big price that was paid to obtain it. God rewards those who diligently seek him and are obedient to his word and he can reward the unjust as well. I do believe that as you read through this book you will gain insight on how Jealousy and Envy operate.

My book can be used as a reference with accompanying scriptures as needed or to share with someone who is going through a difficult time. I chose to use more scriptures from the Touch Point New Living Translation Bible because it is simple to read and understand and it brings about a clearer translation. The King James Version has been used as well. Feel free to compare and read the scriptures from your favorite Bible and pray for the understanding of the word of God. Another Bible of preference for easier understanding is the Amplified Bible. Due to the sensitive nature of Jealousy and Envy, I wanted to be straightforward. I encourage you to read scriptures out loud and make it personal if appropriate for your situation. I hope you will take the information that you receive and share with someone else to be a blessing.

I chose to write about this topic because it is thought of so lightly by people. It is often seen as being harmless or is sometimes used in conversations jokingly with no ill intent, but it can eventually be a seed planted to grow into something bigger and harmful. It harms and destroys relationships, but God is a deliverer and a restorer.

We have to be very careful with what we say about a person and what we do to people. We must also be very cautious about our assumptions and perceptions of people or situations. In my book, I address inappropriate behaviors brought on due to the Killers: Jealousy and Envy.

Note to the Reader: As the reader, any circumstances or situations that may be familiar to you are merely coincidental and do not refer to any specific individuals. It was my intention to write a book that has a universal approach, whereas, anyone could identify with its content.

Chapter One
What Do Jealousy and Envy Mean?

Do any of these questions sound familiar to you? Why didn't I get promoted on my job before they did? Why didn't I get the house, car, or the swimming pool when I attempted to do so? Why didn't I get pregnant after trying so many years and my friend got pregnant after trying one month? Why didn't I lose weight quickly after trying so many diets? If you haven't asked any of these questions then perhaps the next set will be recognizable to you. Why am I not married yet? Why aren't my children obedient and successful? Why haven't I achieved more in life by now? Why didn't I marry him or her? If you have asked any of these questions at some point in despair or discontentment and compared yourself with someone else's situation then there is a chance you were experiencing a taste of Jealousy and Envy without really recognizing it. Questions like these can cross anyone's mind from time to time; however, if someone else has what you desire and you're not happy for them then it's time to evaluate your feelings.

According to Webster's New Collegiate Dictionary, Jealousy is defined as:

Jealousy: 1: A jealous disposition, attitude or feeling 2: zealous vigilance

Jealous: 1. A. Intolerant of rivalry or unfaithfulness: apprehensive of the loss of another's exclusive devotion. 2. Hostile toward a rival or one believed to enjoy an advantage. 3. Vigilant in guarding a possession. 4. Distrustfully watchful.

Envy   1. Malice 2. Painful or resentful awareness of an advantage enjoyed by another joined with a desire to possess the same advantage.

Envious is begrudging another possession of something.

It carries a strong implication of distrust, suspicion, enviousness or sometimes anger.

Envy stresses a coveting of something (as riches or attainments), which belongs to another, or something (as success or good luck), which comes to another; it may imply an urgent, even malicious desire to see another dispossessed.

Jealousy is a common emotion of passion and if one is not delivered from it, this can lead to hatred. Some people are jealous of the way someone looks, what they have achieved, their house, car, business, happy family, talents, and the list goes on and on.

Sometimes we think that High Blood Pressure, Stroke, and Diabetes are the only silent killers in the medical world; however, I am sure that you can think of other ways that people are killed. Have you ever thought about the possibility that you or someone you know may be guilty of killing someone else due to

Jealousy or Envy. Words can destroy a person's reputation the same way as using any type of physical means that one can think of or imagine. Jealousy and Envy are cousins or closely related. They operate in the lives of many across the country daily; with no respect of persons. It doesn't matter who you are, your social status, income, sex, or race. The main objective is to get into your heart, spirit, and soul to destroy and hurt you and others around you. These cousins bring along with them persecution, betrayal, and rejection. Their traits are very similar although somewhat different. However, both can be deadly and painful to relationships and associations. The pain is more severe when it is your brother or sister in Christ. The results can lead to broken relationships, unforgiveness, offenses, and wounds that must heal with time. Once trust is lost it has to be reestablished again, if ever, over time. It is usually easier to forgive the person versus trusting them again. It is easy to forgive those who you don't have to be around; however, it takes a much greater effort to forgive those who you have to see on a daily basis. Forgiveness is something that has to be done in order to move forward in life.

Feelings and Emotions Associated With Jealousy and Envy

1. Betrayal
2. Rejection
3. Sadness
4. Fear
5. Hatred
6. Strife
7. Revenge
8. Suspicion
9. Obsession
10. Insecurity
11. Anger
12. Bitterness
13. Resentment

14. Pride
15. The need to blame
16. Intimidation
17. Isolation

Chapter Two
Biblical Examples of Jealousy and Envy

An example of Envy in the Bible is the story of Cain and Abel, sons of Adam and Eve. Cain killed his brother, Abel, because Abel gave his best gift to God. (Genesis 4:1-8) Cain was the oldest son, and a tiller of the ground (farmer). Abel's job was to tend to sheep. Both had the opportunity to give God their best offering; however, Cain chose not to give his best. Abel gave God his best sheep and Cain became envious of Abel's gift. Cain gave God the spoiled or worst part of his harvest. God was very pleased with Abel's gift but displeased with Cain's gift; therefore, Cain's offering was unacceptable in the sight of God. Cain presented God his left over harvest and did not receive the reaction he desired. He became so affected by the Killers, Jealousy and Envy, that this led him to kill his brother in rage.

Another example is in 1 Samuel 18:1-11. In this story Saul is King. Jonathan and David were so close that they felt that their souls were knitted together by love and respect. Jonathan loved David enough to give him his robe and everything that came along with it to use in battle. Saul was initially impressed with David killing Goliath; however, when David returned from fighting there was so much rejoicing over what David had done that Saul became envious and angry. He began to compare what he had done with what David had done. David had killed more people than Saul. Saul had killed his thousands and David his ten thousands. Saul was afraid of losing his position; therefore, he became angry enough to attempt to kill David with a javelin but didn't succeed.

Genesis 37:1-36 tells the story of Joseph and his encounter with the Evil Twins. Joseph's brothers were jealous of him and hated him because of the favor he had with his father. They sold him into slavery but he ended up being very successful and blessed his brothers.

Another well-known story in the Bible concerns that of Sarai and Hagar. (Genesis chapter 16) Sarai asked her husband, Abraham, to get Hagar pregnant because she was too old and barren. After Hagar conceived and the child was born, Sarai started to despise Hagar. Sarai possessed strong feelings of jealousy and envy toward Hagar; therefore, she treated her badly.

In everyday life, people are jealous and envious because someone has a new house, new job, new car, successful family, new promotion, new clothes, a close relationship with the Lord, and the list goes on and on to include materialistic things as well as unmaterialistic things.

An envious person may not want the house or car; they simply don't want to see the other person have it. Therefore, it is very hard for someone who is envious to be happy for someone else. They would rather wish evil upon that person, see the person fail, or lose what they may have. Usually, there is ill will towards the person for no reason at all. For example, in the workplace or church when an employee or member has been appointed to a position of authority and leadership, an envious person will ask why them and not me? "I am just as good as they are or better." The end result usually is to try to discredit the person. This is very common in today's society. Coworkers might be envious of someone being in a certain position and they do not want to see that particular person in that position; therefore, they do all they can to bring the person down. They don't necessarily want the position, they just don't want to see the other person advance or receive recognition. So they criticize the person's efforts in an attempt to demean the person's character or reputation.

Here are a few verses taken from the New Living Translation found in Galatians to meditate on.

If we are born again and are living by the spirit then the Holy Spirit should control our lives. Galatians 5: 22-23 reads," But when the Holy Spirit controls our lives, he will produce this kind of fruit in us: love, joy, peace, patience, kindness, goodness, faithfulness,… gentleness and self-control. Here there is no conflict with the law."

Galatians 5: 24 "Those who belong to Christ Jesus have nailed the passions and desires of their sinful nature to his cross and crucified them there."

Galatians 5: 25 "If we are living now by the Holy Spirit let us follow the Holy Spirit's leading in every part of our lives. Let us not be conceited, or irritate one another or be jealous of one another."

Chapter Three
Ways in Which Jealousy is Manifested

1. Competitiveness- competition with weight, sports, talents and abilities, A person can be recently promoted, but still want the next position before someone else gets it. Also a person who is competitive always has to be the first to do something or get something before someone else does.

2. Inferiority complex-just doesn't fit in, feeling of rejection and insecurity.

3. Rebellion- Children can be jealous of parents being in a relationship and become rebellious due to the feeling of rejection.

4. Parental Jealousy-Parents can be jealous of a child's relationship with the other parent because the child might feel closer to the other parent due to quality time spent together.

5. Has to make comparisons-Some people overextend themselves by trying to obtain what others may have, how others may look, or even what others may do.

Reasons Why People Become Jealous

1. Low self -esteem- Feelings of not measuring up to others standards. This could be due to being told as a child you're stupid, dumb, you can't do that or be that, you're slow, lazy, ugly, etc. A person who has low self-esteem often craves attention and feels bad if not praised or complimented often by others.

2. Disappointment of present situations or conditions-When things are desired but not manifested quick enough. It seems like it's taking forever to get what is desired and impatience sets in.

3. Resentment- When someone seems more blessed and gets what is desired by what seems to be little or no effort.

4. Rejection-Feels like an outsider, they don't fit in, and something is wrong with them or everyone else. Also due to pride, the person sometimes rejects those who may be able to help them.

5. Don't feel loved or accepted-Didn't grow up in a home where a lot of love and affection was shown, and this can hinder someone from accepting and expressing genuine love.

6. Insecurity-Doesn't know how to trust anyone. Has the need to be with people all the time or in certain groups to cover the lack of security and confidence of being alone.

7. Lack of companionship or friendship-Has a hard time keeping or meeting genuine friends. Always has their guard up. Usually settles for unhealthy relationships.

8. Lack of commitment to God or lack of a committed relationship with God -Usually feels it doesn't take all that and doesn't want to be labeled as a Holy Roller; therefore, will compromise their relationship with God just to be accepted or to fit in with the popular crowd.

9. Conviction-Feels uncomfortable around strong Believers and people of Integrity because the light of God inside the Christian exposes their darkness. They know what is the right thing to do but doesn't do it. Observes True Believers but has to find something negative to say about them in order to make themselves seem okay or to get the focus off them.

10. Past history of childhood trauma due to sibling rivalry- Has poor relationships with their sisters and brothers and feels like one might be the favorite, loved more, or treated differently by their parents or other family members.

11. Wrong Perceptions-Feels that what is felt or assumed is really true when usually it is not. Perceives a person or situation in a wrong way. Makes judgments according to misinformation without facts. Occasionally will find out the truth, but has too much pride to admit that they were wrong. Usually judges things according to their strong feelings.

12. Emotional wounds and pains from a past experience - Someone is hurt from the past and has never gotten over it. Feels that they must hurt others before they hurt them. Feels that sooner or later everybody hurts somebody due to hurt feelings. Is paranoid and feels that someone is out to get them. Usually is miserable and seeks to make others feel the same.

13. Angry and Mean-Lacks the knowledge of how to handle conflicts, therefore, they run from confrontation. When confronted, they allow their feelings to get out of control and then those feelings are displayed through anger.

14. Attention Seekers-Craves recognition, compliments, and always wants a pat on the back.

Chapter Four
What Do Jealous and Envious People Do?

1. Slander- start false rumors, tell lies
2. Try to discredit a person by character assassination
3. Try to break up relationships, marriages, and friendships
4. Resist authority figures- can't submit, are rebellious
5. Try to imitate the person they are jealous of (a carbon copy)
6. Betray a friend or someone close to them
7. Manipulate and control
8. Criticize a person's efforts
9. Very seldom admit there's a problem within them
10. Form or gather allies- Find others that have the same opinion about the person or have to influence others to feel the same way.
11. Mistreat others
12. Compare and compete with others
13. Intimidate others

The reasons people are jealous and envious and what these people do is usually the same. Their motives and actions go hand in hand. It is very hard to talk about one without mentioning the other. These people reject others and persecute them.

The following verses from the King James Version pertains to overcoming persecution:

Matthew 5:10," Blessed are they which are persecuted for righteousness' sake: for theirs is the kingdom of heaven."

Matthew 5:11, "Blessed are ye, when men shall revile you, and persecute you, and say all manner of evil against you FALSELY for my sake. Rejoice, and be exceeding glad: for great is your reward in heaven: for so persecuted they the prophets which were before you."

2 Timothy 3:12 "Yes, and everyone who wants to live a godly life in Christ Jesus will suffer persecution."

Chapter Five
Why Are Christians Persecuted?

1. The attack is to stop the anointing from operating in your life.
2. To make you give up.
3. For you to doubt God's power.
4. Happens because you're doing something right.
5. You have decided to be set apart and not compromise.
6. It shows what you are made of spiritually.

No one knows us better than God and ourselves. If we try, we can figure out why things are happening in our lives. After we do an inventory of our own life, the bottom line should always be, "Am I doing what is right and what is pleasing to God?" We have to always keep our motives pure and honest before God because he sees all and knows all. People can be fooled, but God can never be fooled. You can fool people for a while, but the real you will be revealed eventually. The true tests for any Believer is to ask the question, "Are my actions lining up with the word of God?"

Sometimes the person may be someone closely connected to you or someone that you thought would never hurt you. Have you ever done something for someone and then in return you were persecuted? Therefore always guard your heart. Pray for your enemies and ask God to bless them (allow God to correct them and show them their error) and you will get your reward by remaining a person of integrity. Don't try to take matters into your own hands because God is the avenger, and he will fight your battle. In Romans 12:19 we are told, "Dearly beloved, avenge not yourselves, but rather give place unto wrath: for it is written, Vengeance is mine; I will repay, saith the Lord"(KJV). It might seem like it's taking a long time for things to stop but God has the perfect time for it all to end, and he will do a perfect work in you as well. Out of the circumstance or situation you will become stronger and wiser. Wait patiently and with the right attitude. God always wins. We must fight the good fight of faith and not grow weary. 1 Timothy 6:12 reads," Fight the good fight of faith, lay hold on eternal life, whereunto thou art also called, and hast professed a good profession before many witnesses" (KJV).

Here are a few additional scriptures to mediate on from the King James Version:

Psalms 25:21 "Let integrity and uprightness preserve: for I wait on thee."

Nehemiah 8:10 "The joy of the Lord is my strength."

Matthew 5: 44 "But I say unto you, Love your enemies, bless them that curse you, do good to them that hate you, and pray for them which despitefully use you and persecute you."

2 Samuel 22: 21 "The Lord rewarded me according to my righteousness: according to the cleanness of my hands hath he recompensed me."

Here are additional scriptures from the New Living Translation:

Proverbs 4:23 "Above all else, guard your heart, for it affects everything you do."

Proverbs 4:24 "Avoid all perverse talk; stay far from corrupt speech."

Sometimes the people around you would rather believe a lie about you than the truth because they fear the rejection of man and want to be liked and accepted by everyone. They crave to be popular instead of doing what is right or not being involved. We have to stand for what is right and do what is pleasing to God. We **must** please God. **Pleasing God has to be the top priority in our lives.** He honors us when we please him. We can not compromise or lower our Standards for acceptance. People come and go out of our lives all the time. Some people are only sent to be in our lives for a season. God never leaves us. When in doubt as to who to follow or what to do, refer to Psalms 25: 4-5 which reads," Show me the path where I should walk, O Lord; point out the right road for me to follow. Lead me by your truth and teach me, for you are the God who saves me. All day long I put my hope in you"(NLT).

To those who are being persecuted and rejected, I would like to say "Be strong in the Lord because it is a spiritual battle and you will overcome." **You will come out of the situation you are presently experiencing.** Don't grow weary and give up, especially, when the end result is victory for you. There will be a testimony from your test and you will have a message from all the mess. You will enjoy peace and joy like never before. This test or trial can be used as a time to get to know who you are in the Lord and to learn more about others as well. You will even get to know of God's love, protection, and favor in an extra special way. The battle is not yours, it's the Lord's. During this time, you may feel lonely but you're not alone. God loves you too much to ever leave you.

Remember, If you are a victim of jealousy and envy or if you're victimizing someone else due to such emotions, I would like for you to know that there is hope and you can recover from the wounds.

Consider these scriptures from the King James Version:

Psalms 18:39 "For thou has girded me with strength unto the battle: thou has subdued under me those that rose up against me."

Psalms 18:48 "He delivereth me from mine enemies: yea, thou liftest me up above those that rise up against me: thou has delivered me from the violent man."

Deuteronomy 31:6 "Be strong and of a good courage, fear not, nor be afraid of them: for the Lord thy God, he it is that doth go with thee; he will not fail thee, nor forsake thee."

Most of all, during this time you will learn to not be so concerned with the opinions of others when it's contrary to who you are. I know because I have experienced the victory in my life from the attacks due to Jealousy and Envy. Situations and circumstances have a way of separating us from people for a while, but it is very well worth it. God has to move out all distractions and allow us to make choices in order for him to be able to speak to us, and to lead and guide us. God never goes against our will. However, he lets us make choices and we have to endure the consequences whether good or bad. Being alone might make you feel like you are on a desert or in the wilderness by yourself, but you're not. The outcome will be more wisdom, faith, and an understanding of why it all happened or why you're going through the test or trial. You will be able to hear from God and receive clear instructions and guidance. He will show you things that you need to know. He will even confirm some things about the situation that you already know.

I was brought up in a Christian home which was a loving, safe, and secure environment. My siblings and I were taught to treat everybody right, do well unto others, and be happy for others when they accomplish something. We were taught that charity starts at home. I thought that everyone was taught the same thing, but I found out through life experiences that everyone wasn't raised the same. There are people who don't like or love themselves so they have a challenge loving or showing love to others. I was to some degree naïve about things because I had to learn that sometimes people don't always do you right, they're not always happy for you, and they will go to whatever extent necessary to discredit you due to their own jealousy. I learned this through my young adult and adult life. When raised as a PK (Preacher's Kid) sometimes people will have unrealistic expectations and make assumptions about you such as, you think you're better than the next person, but that is not true. Preacher kids are human too. I had to practice the Godly lessons I was taught using the Word to overcome the trials and tests of life in order to get the victory. Although my parents left a legacy of love, as I was going through, I didn't feel like loving those who hurt me but I knew I had to do what the word said to do. I do not regret anything that I have been through because it has made me more bolder and stronger. I am just so thankful that I endured with victory through my trials and tribulations. I have learned about longsuffering, patience, mercy, and grace because of the things I went through.

I learned I couldn't fight with natural means like the other people who had hurt me, but I could fight the good fight of faith by believing that God would help me through it. I prayed for them, blessed them, showed them agape love, and most of all, I continued to diligently serve the Lord with all my heart because

I felt deep down inside that God was bragging on me. I started thanking and praising him even before I came out of the situation. I learned how to worship God and to keep a pure heart before him. He was my guide, my friend, and comforter. As I was going through the trials and tests, I kept confessing who God said that I am. As a victim, you have to know for yourself who you are no matter how much you are persecuted. It does hurt when people lie on you and those who know the truth don't stand up for what is right due to intimidation. If you are hurting or in pain due to the result of someone else's emotions or insecurities, I would like to say that "the pain is temporary and God is a Healer of broken hearts." **Sometimes you can hurt so bad that the last thing that you want to do is to think about praying, but you have to.** When you can't pray with words then pray in the spirit. You won't know what you are praying but God will know. You can also pray for an understanding. You will immediately feel your strength coming back and a renewal of your mind. Sometimes you might want to cry but can't. It is okay to cry because crying brings about a cleansing to the body; however, excessive and uncontrollable crying is unhealthy. At all cost, avoid self-pity. God will wipe away the tears and turn your tears into joy. According to Psalms 126:5, "They that sow in tears shall reap in joy"(KJV). And Psalms 56:8 tells us, "You keep track of all my sorrows. You have collected all my tears in a bottle. You have recorded each one in your book"(KJV).

God will give you joy. Joy will be your strength. Joy was my strength to endure the test and trials. Sometimes fear might want to grab a hold of you, but fear not and don't be afraid of anything someone could say or do. Remember, Hebrews 13:6 states," So that we may boldly say, The Lord is my helper, and I will not fear what man shall do unto me" (KJV).

The greatest weapon is to love the person, continue to ask God to bless them, and to show them their error or what they are doing wrong. Admit to God your true feelings about the situation you're in and guard your heart. **It's okay to be angry; however, you can't remain that way.** Don't try to deny it. In the natural you might even, want to fight back physically but you can't. You might be tempted to get even but that wouldn't be the right thing either. You have to cast down those thoughts and think on the positive things. This isn't always so easy at first but the more you practice it, it will become easier. I say to you as my friend, Grace, has always told me," Just be still and watch God move.' 'He has everything under control."

Being happy is situational. It can change from moment to moment but Joy is constant. Even though things might be rough, there has to be joy on the inside to let you know things are going to be all right. If the person who you might have a problem with is a sinner or isn't born again then pray for their salvation, deliverance, and wholeness. (Sinner's Confession) Roman 10:9 states, " That if thou shall confess with thou mouth the Lord Jesus, and shalt believe in thine heart that God has raised him from the dead, thou shall be saved"(KJV). When I was being mistreated and persecuted, I was held safely in the arms of God and he carried me when I felt like I couldn't go on any further. He never left me nor did he forsake me. He comforted me and assured me that he had everything in control and all I had to do was to be still, wait, rest, and trust in him. The pain is only temporary. Think of it as a test and a learning experience.

If you are someone who victimizes by persecuting and lying on others, I would like for you to know that you can capture your emotions and cease from being jealous and envious. Just admit your feelings. Think about how you would feel if someone was doing the same thing to you.

My parents used to always tell us to remember that when people don't love themselves, it is hard for them to love others. Love has to be given in order to receive it. Learn to love yourself and then you can sow seeds of Love. Galatians 6:7 states, "Be not deceived; God is not mocked: for whatsoever a man soweth, that shall he also reap"(KJV).

St. John 13:34 declares," A new commandment I give unto you, that ye love one another; as I have loved you, that ye also love one another" (KJV).

Romans 13:10 also states, " Love worketh no ill to his neighbor: therefore love is the fulfilling of the law" (KJV).

Most of the time, hurting people hurt others. Think about your motives and the consequences. Is what you're doing really worth the cost of a broken friendship whether it is personal, church, or business related? Jealousy and Envy both operate in homes, schools, churches and the workplace. I plea to you to take a second look at what is being said about or done to someone else due to your perception of the person. Sometimes a perception of a particular situation or person can be entirely different from how something really is. To assume something about a person without knowing the facts can cause a lot of problems and hurt feelings.

Chapter Six
Eight Steps to Overcoming Jealousy and Envy

1. Admit it to yourself and sometimes to the person you're jealous of and also repent.
2. Seek God's Guidance and Godly counsel from a mentor or seasoned believer.
3. Pray and Fast
4. Read and confess deliverance scriptures daily.
5. Be able to receive constructive criticism in order to receive deliverance.
6. Be happy about someone else's success and find out how they obtained success.
7. Give thanks for your deliverance and be a witness to someone else. - Don't let condemnation set in and don't let pride keep you from telling your testimony.
8. Ask for forgiveness and forgive yourself.

Scriptures from the New Living Translation

Proverbs 23:17-18   "Don't envy sinners, but always continue to fear the Lord. For surely you have a future ahead of you; your hope will not be disappointed."

Proverbs 3:31   "Do not envy violent people; don't copy their ways."

Proverbs 27:4   "Anger is cruel, and wrath is like a flood, but who can survive the destructiveness of Jealousy?"

Ephesians 4:32   " Instead, be kind to each other, tenderhearted, forgiving one another, just as God through Christ has forgiven you."

Galatians 5:26 "Let us not become conceited, or irritate one another, or be jealous of one another."

James 3:16   "For wherever there is jealousy and selfish ambition, there you will find disorder and every kind of evil."

1 Peter 2:1 " So get rid of all malicious behavior and deceit. Don't just pretend to be good! Be done with hypocrisy and jealousy and backstabbing."

Psalms 103:11-12 "For his unfailing love towards those who fear him is as great as the height of the heavens above the earth. He has removed our rebellious acts as far away from us as the east is from the west."

Romans 8:1 " So now there is no condemnation for those who belong to Christ Jesus."

Romans 12:2 "Don't copy the behavior and customs of this world, but let God transform you into a new person by changing the way you think. Then you will know what God wants you to do, and you will know how good and pleasing and perfect his will really is."

James 1:3-4 "For when your faith is tested, your endurance has a chance to grow; so let it grow, for when endurance is fully developed, you will be strong in character and ready for anything."

1 Peter 1:7 "These trials are only to test your faith, to show that it is strong and pure. It is being tested as fire and purifies gold- and your faith is far more precious to God than mere gold. So if your faith remains strong after being tried by fiery trials, it will bring you much praise and glory and honor on the day when Jesus Christ is revealed in the whole world."

Prayer for Deliverance from Jealousy and Envy

Father God, in Jesus Name, I ask you to root out every inch of jealousy or envy that would try to operate in my life. Forgive me. I repent. I realize that jealousy and envy cripples and hinders me from walking in your divine will, health, and fullness of life. I ask you to restore my soul and give me a new beginning in Jesus Name. Help me to receive forgiveness and to forgive others. I thank you for a new beginning. In Jesus name, Amen.

Prayer for Anger

Father, in the name of Jesus, I admit the anger I feel and I repent of it. I ask you to remove this anger and replace it with your love and kindness. I ask for self –control to operate in my life daily, now and forever. I thank you for the grace to do it. In Jesus name, Amen.

Prayer for Bitterness and Resentment

Father God, in the name of Jesus, I ask you to remove all bitterness and resentment from my heart right now, so that I can be set free and restore unto me a clean and pure heart. I plead the blood of Jesus over my life and every emotion in Jesus name. Thanks for answering my prayer, Amen.

Meditation Scripture for Bitterness and Resentment

Ephesians 4:31-32 "Let all bitterness, and wrath, and anger, and clamour, and evil speaking, be put away from you, with all malice, and be ye kind one to another, tenderhearted, forgiving one another, even as God for Christ's sake hath forgiven you"(KJV).

Note to the reader: Please feel free to substitute any feelings or emotions in the above prayers.

Chapter Seven
Words of Encouragement

If somehow you have been faced with Jealousy and Envy or is in a present battle with it, I would like for you to know that there is help. If the result is that you're hurting or in despair, I say to you to look up and live. God made you unique and he can heal a broken heart. Psalms 34:18 reminds us that, "The Lord is nigh unto them that are of a broken heart; and saveth such as be of a contrite spirit"(KJV). **He has a special place for you in life. There's a work for you to do and only you can do it.** Don't strive to be a copy when God has made us all originals. **We are to imitate Christ.** You are victorious and more than a conqueror. God loves you and he cares for you. He wants to deliver you so you can help others. According to Psalms 86: 11, we should pray," Teach me thy way, O Lord; I will walk in thy truth: unite my heart to fear thy name" (KJV).

Jealousy and Envy wound and destroy lives and relationships. However, God loves you and you can get victory over these killers of your emotions and passions. Restoration is inevitable once the choice is made to change. Instead of letting these two things

47

operate in your life, remember Philippians 4:8 reads," Finally, brethren, whatsoever things are true, whatsoever things are honest, whatsoever things are just, whatsoever things are pure, whatsoever things are lovely, whatsoever things are of good report; if there be any virtue, and if there be any praise, think on these things" (KJV).

When you're jealous of someone else you're really saying that God made you to be not good enough. We are a masterpiece and wonderfully made. We need to be the very best that we can be to fulfill our mission here on earth. When we admire people for who they are and learn to celebrate their victories, we have won the battle in our minds against the killers Jealousy and Envy. True rewards come from being able to appreciate and celebrate another person's season of blessings.

If you have been a victim or victorious in overcoming Jealousy and Envy, I ask you to reach out and help someone else to overcome these Killers. Plant the seeds of love and compassion because God is love. God's love is unconditional. He loves us in spite of what we may have done. Acts 3: 19 states," Repent ye therefore, and be converted, that your sins may be blotted out, when the times of refreshing shall come from the presence of the Lord" (KJV). God only requires that we repent and turn away from doing whatever is not pleasing to him and to move forward towards His blessings and prosperity. When we truly repent from something, our actions change and we don't have to continue to do what is wrong. There doesn't have to be a continuous asking for forgiveness for the same thing over and over again. When sincere and genuine repentance occurs, there is so much peace and joy for everyone involved in the test or trial. St. Luke 15 v. 10 tells us, " Likewise, I say unto you, there is joy in the presence of the angels of God over one sinner that repenteth" (KJV).

Love is the key to your victory. God will shower us with blessings in every area of our lives. Love does no wrong to anyone. **Love will not allow us to be jealous and envious of anyone.** Love will not let us persecute or betray anyone. God has a plan for each of us. He made us and knows all about us. He knows where we are and where we are headed. According to Psalms 139:14, "I will praise thee; for I am fearfully and wonderfully made: marvelous are thy works; and that my soul knoweth right well" (KJV). Furthermore, Ephesians 1: 4-6 read, "According as he hath chosen us in him before the foundation of the world, that we should be holy and without blame before him in love: Having predestinated us unto the adoption of children by Jesus Christ to himself, according to the good pleasure of his will to the praise of the glory of his grace, wherein he hath made us accepted in the beloved" (KJV).

When one gains the victory over Envy and Jealousy one can declare Psalms 118:23," this is the Lord's doing; it is marvelous in our eyes" (KJV). To God be the Glory!

"Why Should One Man Be Jealous Of Another?"
Poem by Lamont Thompson

The Lord says to love one another as if he was your own brother.
In some cases Jealousy and Envy are the cause of someone's wants and not their needs.
So in other words, these feelings are not of the Lord but are brought on from greed.
Brought from selfishness that eats upon one's soul,
And this causes the blessings that God has in store for you, to be put on hold.
To be Jealous and Envious is not of God, but love and respect is what we should do.
So you should be patient and understanding, because God has a divine plan ordained just for you.

Chapter Eight
Conclusion

I have shared a lot of scriptures that will serve as comfort and healing. When going through tests and trials, pray and reflect back on some of these scriptures. I used them when I was going through difficult times and I got the victory through the Word. I continue to meditate on the word in order to be prepared for the next spiritual battle. **Through it all, God has been good to me!** His grace and mercy brought me through it all. I have learned to lean, trust, and depend on God like never before. My faith is stronger, and I know the true meaning of praise and worship; therefore, I have developed an intimate relationship with the Lord: **I know not to compromise or give in. With God on my side, I always win.** I am very thankful that he chose me to be worthy of his love, mercy, and kindness. I have a sincere desire to see others set free and delivered. If you don't know Jesus as your personal Lord and saviour please accept him and let him come into your heart today. God's love conquers all.

I find it appropriate to leave you with the Love chapter from the New Living Translation Touchpoint Bible, 1 Corinthians 13:1-13 reads,

"If I could speak in any language in heaven or on earth but didn't love others, I would only be making meaningless noise like a loud gong or clanging cymbal.

If I had the gift of prophecy, and if I knew all the mysteries of the future and knew everything about everything, but didn't love others, what good would I be? And if I had the gift of faith so that I could speak to a mountain and make it move, without love I would be no good to anybody.

If I gave everything I have to the poor and even sacrificed my body, I could boast about it, but if I didn't love others, I would be of no value whatsoever.

Love is patient and kind. Love is not jealous or boastful or proud or rude. Love does not demand it's own way. Love is not irritable, and it keeps no record of when it has been wronged.

It is never glad about injustice but rejoices when the truth wins out.

Love never gives up, never loses faith, is always hopeful, and endures through every circumstance.

Love will last forever, but prophecy and speaking in unknown languages and special knowledge will all disappear.

Now we know only a little, and even the gift of prophecy reveals little!

But when the end comes, these special gifts will all disappear.

It's like this: when I was a child, I spoke and thought and reasoned as a child does. But when I grew up, I put away childish things.

Now we see things imperfectly as in a poor mirror, but then we will see everything with perfect clarity.

All that I know now is partial and incomplete, but then I will know everything completely, just as God know me now.

There are three things that will endure- faith, hope and love- and the greatest is love."

enlighten you on why people
are jealous or envy. Some of the
things they do because of this spirit
if you are a victim or have
been ~~into~~ victimized by these two
evils you can be delivered. There
are scriptures to help you
overcome.

Final Thoughts

I have a deep passion for this subject because I have seen how it destroys relationships. It is my desire that my book will bring about a life changing experience for the reader and that the scriptures will bring comfort, hope, and deliverance.

I have learned about unconditional love: Loving someone inspite of their actions or conditions. I have truly learned to love the unlovely. It's easy to love the lovely but the greatest victory is loving the unlovable, which takes a **whole lot** of prayer and effort. If we practice unconditional love, there's no way that Killers like Jealousy and Envy can exist in our lives, workplace, homes, schools, churches, etc. **Remember, the greatest weapon is Love.**

To order additional copies of

Jealousy or Envy: Is There a Killer in You?

have your credit card ready and call
1 800-917-BOOK (2665)

or e-mail
orders@selahbooks.com

or order online at
www.selahbooks.com

The Author can be contacted directly by:

Email:
lindathompson47@bellsouth.net

Phone:
(919) 751-8063